IRKI

KADIJA SESAY

IRKI

PEEPAL TREE

First published in Great Britain in 2013
Peepal Tree Press Ltd
17 King's Avenue
Leeds LS6 1QS
UK

ISBN 13: 9781845232085

Supported using public funding by
ARTS COUNCIL
ENGLAND

ACKNOWLEDGEMENTS

To my parents for always making sure that we had as many good books to eat as we had good food. To sister Saffi and husband Mark for always being there, with love and support without judgement or pause. To my brother Olu, for the memories.

Many, many thanks to the El Gouna Writer's Residency in Egypt which allowed me to treat myself as a writer, instead of an editor/publisher and so able to be an activist for myself, for a month. Thank you to the writers who shared my El Gouna experience: Maggie Gee, Abdullah al Khafri, Hillary Jordan, Nick Rankin, and Victor Torres whose warm company gave me renewed spirit, motivation and belief to work on my writing. Shukran.

To Dorothea Smartt for her friendship and constant encouragement in not allowing me to escape reading publicly whenever the opportunity presents itself.

Heather Taylor, one of the first people to give me their time and energy on SABLE, whose poems about her grandmothers inspired me to write mine, so becoming the start of this collection.

Friends Julia, Cathy, Sharon and Diane who I met at John Howard Grammar School for Girls on the first day – thank you for remaining my friends.

Don Kinch for publishing my first poem, in *Staunch*, a poem that came from an amazing trip to Trinidad, organised by the late Ossie and Ruby Nobelmunn who spent the best part of their lives working with and encouraging youth.

Ade Daramy for not realising he was going to be my Krio translator and being so gracious with his time at short notice.

Janet Poynting whose beautiful knitting reminded me how much knitting once featured in my life, now here, in some of the poems.

To Viccy Arana, Maria Lima, Libby Hodges (*St Petersburg Review*), thank you for your gentle, constant support. Kamau Brathwaite, Jack Mapanje and Niyi Osundare for continued prodding and encouragement to reveal my poems – done it now – ok!

The Etteridges, the family who took care of myself and my siblings when we were children. To other children who were privately fostered; particularly for those who did not have a good experience – this is only part of the story, please tell your stories.

To my other families who have all, in some way helped this collection come into being: Phila Family: Auntie Giftie, Claude, David, Leslie, Samuela, Lena et al.; Washington DC Family: Juliette Bethea, "my man in DC" Clayton Spitzer, Koye Oyedeji and Montre Azzouri, Juanita and Mel Hardy, (late) Clement Goddard; Nubian Family in Egypt: Mr Markab, Mr Hamdi et al.; Tunisia Family: where the book really started to take shape, Wangui wa Goro, Suzie Teete, Moez and Mahdi (thanks for letting me stay at your beautiful house) and especially the unforgettable Chadly; Peepal Tree Family (of course!): Hannah, thank you for taking my book seriously and producing it so beautifully; Jeremy for the scary, but totally essential to-the-point editing. Thank you for helping to make it less scary! And finally, once again to my sister, Saffi and husband Mark, thank you can never be enough. To anyone I have left out of my "thank yous and acknowledgements" – understand that now I've reached that middle-age moment, I've inherited "the beauty of forgetting" – sorry!

The following earlier versions of poems have been previously published: "Queen of Ol' Wharf" in Dance The Guns to Silence, flipped eye publishing, UK (November, 2005); "Pink Shoes" in Northern Lights, (Leeds What's On Guide, 2006); "Grandmothers I"; "Grandmothers II", in Drum Voices Revue (SIUE, 2007); "Shoots" in St. Petersburg Review, NY (2008).

The focus within the "Rituals" section talks of the occurrence of "private fostering". Private fostering was common amongst parents of West African origin, who migrated to the UK in the '50s and '60s. They often placed their children with English families to care for them, for reasons often related to work and or study schedules and living in places unsuitable to raise their children. The experience of children placed with foster families varied greatly, from the foster families informally "adopting" children into loving families to ones of extreme abuse. Regulations in regards to private fostering, are more rigorous today. http://www.privatefostering.org.uk/

CONTENTS

PART 1

LETTING GO

ODE TO *SS ACCRA*
(and her sisters)

I saw three ships come sailing in...

Accra, *Apapa* and *Aureol*,
vessels built for Liverpool,

a fleet of Elder Dempster ships,
signatures of West African trips.

Passenger grips packed with dreams
began to unravel slowly in reams.

Hopes filtered through fingers like sand
blown away with memories of homeland.

Minds changed with the English weather
but return tickets were never

an option. Headlines: "Wogs, here to stay!"
Maybe they would return home, one day.

LETTING GO: I

This man is the one you say will take care of you?
Feed you? Clothe you? Shelter you? Respect you?
Will not damage you and be a good father to your children?
Inshallah. Okay then, if you say so, I will let you go.

LETTING GO: II

He's on the plane, going; I can't stop him, let him go!
Maybe, he will be better off, maybe;
make some money,
send me pound sterling.

But I don't know, you know,
about this girl he is marrying
from up country.

She's not Methodist;
her family not even Christian,
but she did go to missionary school.

How does he know her?
I tried hard to meet the family;
I know nothing of her history.

Why does my son want to marry her?
She's not so pretty;
typical broad Mende face!

Wit' Krio titi ar no say, ee go pray to me same God.
Muslim man dem? Mmm, ar noh so sure.
Den say Allah na di same —
So oos wan mi granpickin dem go pray to?

GRANDMOTHERS MEETING FOR THE FIRST TIME

Sissy Mariama,
kushe.
How body? Ow di go dae go?
We geh foh tok oh,
becos dis you pikin, sen mi son go fa way.
E say e dae go London.
E no mek sense foh go waaay yanda if no foh yu gyal pikin.
Wetin mek yu no hol' am, eh?
Na wetin e give am for cham?
I don tel am say, no eat outside yu mammy een ose,
but bobo dem, dehn noh dae lis-tin.
Wen e small, I noh get no problem wit um, na good boy pikin,
fase wata, do lili woke fo pay een yone school fee wey me no get um,
ee fen money foh it foh een broddah ehn sista dem.
I wan know, oos kanaba rubbish e put insai een it?
You na de mammy – nah yu I geh foh cam to.

Sissy Modu,
Salam alaikum.
Kushe, kushe,
Ow body?
De body fine, me sista
Ta Barruk Allah.
No bring yu god to me-o! Na me get me god!
I don gee mi gyal pikin to famble insi Freetong, loooong since.
Nah to im cousin e ose, na dey ee bin tap, wey ee meet yu boy pikin.
Ar noh no natin, teey, wey een papa tell me say, e geh for marade.
Na een daddy pwell am, yes. E mek ee go school!
E dae go Inglan, afta wan year pass, nah so ee tell me,
afta yu son mek place for am.
Yu dey yerri me, Sissy Modu?
Ya Allah!
Noh to me-o! Me nah de mammy noh moh, ar noh geh ahn dae!

Ar tap up upline, to Koindu – me? Na de foss tem dis, ar pas Kailahun sef,
me noh no natin wey you dae tok bot.
Wanss ee lef me ose, ar noh no am sef.
Yu boy pikin, noh cam see me sef!
Tings don change-o!
Wa' mek yu train yu boy pikin so?
Rahim Allah!
Tek tem-o!
Noh mek ah cam slap yu-o!, Si Mariama
Noh to me bring dis plaba.
Do ya, ar baeg!
Ya Allah! Na confuse ar don confuse!

Wetin I don tell yu? Yu no yeeri ar say, noh bring yu god to me-o!
Tek yu god, tek yu gyal pikin, tek yu plaba!
Na dis kine bizness, mek mami dee die, mek dis worl change! Hmm.

Rahim Allah!

GRANDMOTHERS' MEETING FOR THE FIRST TIME
(English Version)

Sister Mariama,
greetings.
How are you? How is it going? How are things?
We have to talk, you know.
Because of your child, my son is going far away.
He says he's going to London.
It doesn't make sense for him to go so far; it must be because of your daughter.
Why is she so wayward?
What did she give him to eat?
I've told him, time and time again — don't eat outside your mother's house but boys, they don't listen.
When he was small, he never gave me any problems; he was a good boy. He fetched water, did odd jobs to pay his own school fees when I didn't have the money, he found the money for me to feed his brothers and sisters; so, I want to know, what kind of evil did she put in his food?
You are her mother, so you should know.

Sister Modu,
may peace be upon you.
Greetings.
How are you?
I'm fine, sister, thank you.
Blessed is Allah
Don't bring your god here, I have my own god!
My daughter came to live with family in Freetown a long time ago. She has been living at her cousin's house – that is where your son met her.
I didn't know anything until her father told me that she was getting married.
It's her father's fault; he spoilt her. He allowed her to go to school! He told me that she's going to England, in a year's time once your son

has sorted everything out for them.

Are you listening to me, Sister Modu?

Oh Allah!

I'm telling you – it's not my fault! I'm only her mother – I don't have any say in the matter.

I live upline in Koindu. This is my first time to even travel further than Kailahun so I really don't know what you're talking about, because once she left my house, that was it, I hardly saw her;

and as for your son, he never even came to see me.

Things have changed!

Is that the way you have raised your son?

May Allah have mercy on you.

Be careful what you say – I don't want to have to slap you, Sister Mariama.
Please! I didn't cause this trouble.

Oh Allah! I'm just confused by the whole thing myself!

What did I tell you? Didn't you hear me say not to bring your god here? Take your god, take your daughter, take your problems and get out of here. This is the kind of situation that kills mothers, that makes the world upside down. Hmm…

May Allah bless you.

GRANDMOTHERS: I

One chose to lie flat on her narrow wooden bed,
declared, "I won't be getting up anymore."

One tried to lie quietly in her castle
through the terror of a civil war.

Grandmother church, grandmother mosque,
gave up their children to the empire.

One to lie flat on a wooden park bench
in London's Turnham Green.

One to lie on a mattress to yield babies
in exchange for love and dreams.

UNCIVILISED

You know Africans
still swing from
trees where they
come from,
don't you?
That's where
we found
'em.
We 'elped 'em
by bringing 'em 'ere;
cheap to feed;
they only eat rice,
or mashed pota'a
with bu'er.
They don't
use no knife,
not needed for
uncivilised buggers,
they eat with their
'ands
they do –
like monkeys.

Have you seen
the Tarzan flims?
Well, it's true,
that's how
Africans live.
They swing from
trees
instead of walking.
They're all
speaky-spoky
but don't even know
what ackee and saltfish
is! We come from
Africa like them
but they
shtupid – don't know
their own history,
don't want
to believe
they sold
their own people.
Uncivilised.

Keep away from
the West Indians,
especially the
Jamaicans;
they are trouble –
thieves,
unkempt,
knotted hair.
Hemp
smokers.
No eat their
food, oh!
They like
corned beef
but since they
can't afford it,
they buy
cat food instead.
Same thing to them
because they are
uncivilised
slaves.

STREETS OF GOLD

Streets of gold, they promised.

Empty cigarette packets
lined with gold foil,
silver ones too! Generous Britain –
take as much as you like!

Phillip Morris handed us a broom.

BUS ETIQUETTE

I

"Can you take my bag please, as I step onto this bus?"
I look at the sign above the pew, facing-seats;
"Please give up this seat for elderly and pregnant women…"

One stares at my face; another stares at my belly.
I'm sure he will move…
One holds the *Daily Mirror* up pretending he cannot see me…

A woman turns her head sideways –
to face straight in front ; I hope –
God forgive me – that her neck gets a crick.

I put the heavy paper bags between my legs.
"Don't put them there, love,
you're stopping people from getting 'orf ."

Now that he has validated their rudeness,
the one looking at my belly can challenge my eyes;
the one challenging my face now grins, ugly.

II

My 2lb bag of rice, 2 onions, 1 plantain, yam – small – width of my
wrist: I will make them stretch – to last me and my husband one
week.

I looked for "tommies" in a box the market-holder was going to
throw away, and bought pork because it's the cheapest meat I could
find – so expensive.

I will pray to God to forgive me for eating unholy meat;
I only have few shillings left for electricity – he must know
how hard it is here!

I don't see ugly face stand; his foot – by accident – kicks my shopping
over before I have time to pick it up, my tomatoes, rolling down the
aisle…

… Everyone looks down at my veg – then looks away. Conductor
angrily: "See – I told ya! Don't ya un'erstand English? Nah, oo's going
to clear up this mess?"

PARAFFIN BABIES

How many second generation Black British
were conceived in front of a paraffin heater?
Blue for boys; pink for girls.

BACK IN THE DAY

Singers in the 60s
sold thin, plastic, round plates
of black gold –
country, gospel, ska, soul –
Jim Reeves, Ray Charles, Desmond Dekker, Sam Cooke;
young Afro-Caribbeans shimmied,
twisted ankles,
swiped soles of feet
spun waists
stepped to Ska
and swayed to Skeeter,
singing each note clear across
the ocean they'd left and…
… maybe one day their dreams would come true!
"You can get it if you really want…
but you must try…
(…try and try, try and try…)
you'll succeed at last…"*

*"You Can Get It If You Really Want" – song title and lyrics by Jimmy
Cliff, released 1972.

THE BOG

1958

The only thing that made us equal
was our shit – the same colour.
I know because I had to clean it up six days of the week.

They used hard bits of paper – shiny on one side – to wipe their arses,
then dropped it on the floor and in the urinals.
I'm sure this was the true meaning of walking around with shit in your pants.

One fat arse flicked tuppence into the toilet
on top of his shit: "Piece of gold there, nigger,"
took my hand and forced it down the bowl to get it out.

"This is what you came for, ain't it?"

2008

The first thing that most of them come in and do is
vomit – on the floor – as if it is the toilet bowl.

So I've added mouthwash to my line of toiletries –
for anyone to use, although it seems they prefer
to cover their stench with more alcohol.

They use my perfume, my deodorant,
I buff their nails but they don't want to pay for it.
I don't ask for much, just a tip.

One fat club owner said we don't fit their brand.
Another – "we are a good 'thing' – especially at weekends."
The customers just treat and talk to us like shit.

No, we are not equals.

PART 2

RITUALS

'AIR

Fe-e-e-el this!
Go on!
Fe-e-e-el it!

Soft 'n' wiry all at the same time –
'ow do you people ge' your 'air like tha'?
You people?
Yeah – you culud people.
'Ow am I gonna ge' a brush frew tha'?
Tuf' innit?
Bounces back – all springy.
Listen, wha' I'll do for you, love, is,
after I wash i', if it gets any tuffa,
I'll ge' some scissors,
cu' it all orf – might grow back straight 'n'
nice'n'long – then I can brush i'
like me gels 'air.
No extra – a-a-a.
Alrigh'?

Gawd Blimey!
Fe-e-e-el this!

FAMILY RITUALS

Bath ritual.
Three little dark-skinned bodies
scrubbed down once a week
in shared water to remove
the scum of ignorance.

Ironing ritual.
Sheets, shirts, high on starch
and fabric conditioner.
Towels and hankies folded –
but can never get the corners to meet
like Mum can.

Roast rituals.
Lamb goes with mint sauce.
Pork with apple sauce.
Beef with horseradish sauce.
Bread goes with dripping.
And chips go with custard.

TREACLE

Dark treacle or black treacle
has a distinctively strong flavour,
slightly bitter, and a richer colour than golden syrup.
                              (Wikipedia)

My foster dad talked like "Pub Landlord". Called me "Treacle",
his sugar and sweetness, his chocolate button;
he gripped his glass of lager like Pub Landlord too.

Taller and wider than him, he strode up roads, down stairs;
dismissed from the army because his inner ear lopsided him,
the training from those teenage years remained.

Ne'er mind. It gave me a childhood filled with swapping smiles,
treats and secrets, milk teeth to falsies – till one day, it all turned sour.

LORRY DRIVER

Pete's Café was our halfway stop on the motorway.
Dad carried me in, "chocolate button", half asleep;
sat me up on a wooden bench, on two cushions propping bum and legs,
served yokey-egg, pork sausage, fried white bread, baked beans
and tomatoes (pushed to the edge) on a chipped white plate.
Mug of tea, with two sugars, to dip buttered toast in
before being carried back, like Santa Claus's sack – burping.
I sat in my warm nest, between me dad, the driver,
and the other passenger, me bruvva.
My half-term holiday treat.

SUNDAY SCHOOL, SUNDAY ROAST

I

Sunday school.
Where we learned about Mary, Joseph and Baby Jesus.
At birth, he already had a title.

Sunday roast!
My mouth juiced-up with saliva at the imagined smell
of Mum's dinner on the table.

Never chicken –
that was midweek – would it be slicesofwell-donebeefwithYorkshirepud?
Or pork with chewy crackling?

Meat juice
made roast 'taters golden – I dreamed of them as I sang out of tune.
Lamb with mint sauce!

II

Sing Hosanna!
Sing Roast Dinner!
Sing Roast Dinner
To the King of Peas!

Sing Hosanna!
Sing Roast Dinner!
Sing Roast Dinner
To Mushy Peas!

Give me joy in my heart
Give me dumpling
Give me joy in my heart I pray

Give me joy on my plate
Keep me thirsting
Keep me gasping
For apple dumpling all day.

III

Lucky us!
After guitar sing-a-longs and Bible stories, we didn't have far to run.
Our house was opposite the church.

Apple dumpling –
my fave! Hot and gooey – I shoved a big scoop into my mouth – apple side up.
Then couldn't pull the spoon out.

Hard choice –
burnt mouth or a bellyfullofappledumplingwithcustard.
The smell went behind my roof, out my nose.

Prayed hard
for God to release me from this pain – and *he did* speak to me that Sunday –
"Release the apple dumpling!"

It was obvious to me then that God had never tasted apple dumpling,
and I never believed in Sunday school in quite the same way, after that.

NANNA

After Nanna helped Mum cook Sunday roast,
she let me climb on her lap.

Nanna tickled me, played with my hair.
She gave up trying to plait it; too springy, she said.

She helped me bake fairy cakes,
sprinkled with hundreds and thousands.

She always let me pick off the pink ones,
leaving dents like mice footprints in the icing.

When my hands got tired of mixing, hers took over,
white hands veined pink, to match the colour of her hair.

She let me lick the wooden spoon – clean.
And the bowl – nose and chin plastered with cake-mix.

She was always round our house was Nanna,
to give us big smiles, big hugs, big love.

OF THE MANY USES OF VASELINE

His head stuck between metal railings,
ears splayed broad like handles;
neighbour's kids shouted and spat in his face,
"Monkey!" as he waited to be rescued.

Hands around his waist, we tried
to yank his torso from behind,
pushing his forehead from the front.
"I'm hungry", he said as I wiped his cheek.

"Mum!" he shouted,
(for which one, I wasn't sure).
Wasn't there anything we could use
that wouldn't damage his brain?

"Vaseline!" Real Mum had given Mum a full jar
for my dry scalp and crocodile-skin legs.
We used it all that day on me bruvva's big ears,
big head. And to hide the stain of phlegm.

ANGELA

(easter @3)
My brother brought his fiancée home.
She had blonde hair, blue eyes;
she played with me,
lifted me high.
He sang her name
An-ge-la!

(christmas@3)
My real dad brought me a doll home,
almost as big as me with
hard plastic legs,
rubber arms that didn't bend,
thick brown hair – tough to brush –
blue eyes; she sang nursery rhymes.
I named her Angela.

(easter@4)
My real mum brought me the best present ever –
a beautiful brown dolly
with dimples!
"Let me hold her!"
She cried real tears,
made real laughing noises.
I loved this one the best!
My sister, Angela.

GO-KARTING

4 wheels from a doll's pram,
taken off my birthday present
from real Mum and Dad.
"Promise to give them back!"

3-foot plank of wood
found in Dad's shed –
we didn't care about splinters!
His finger warned us,
"Don't get into trouble!"

2 feet length of string
given to us by Mum
that she kept in her knitting box
(for some reason).

1 pair of hands
steering 'round the sloping corner.
Sister, riding pillion, gets her leg caught
between wood and wheel.

1 helluva smacking!

AIRMAIL LETTER

Dear Granny Cole,

I hope this letter finds you as well as we all are here.
Today at school, we had to draw a picture of our grannies.

Teacher said, "What does your grandmother look like?"
I said my granny's nose twitches – a bit like The Grinch.

Teacher said, "What does your grandmother smell like?"
Smell like? I said mine smelt like paper – thin, icy-blue paper.

My friends in the class all said *their* granny's baked cakes.
Granny, can you send me a cake, please?

Can you put green icing on top,
With hundreds of thousands – no, can I have more?

My nanna bakes cakes, but that doesn't count, does it?
Is it ok with you if Nanna is my granny as well?

I ripped up my drawing. Teacher told me off,
said I had to stand in the corner for being naughty.

Sorry, Granny Cole. I'll write more next time.

Lots of love.
God Bless.

VICAR'S BOY

Tongue pink and hanging out,
Peter picked up the scissors
we used in arts and crafts class,
stuck with chipped bits
of pink and blue sugar-paper,
cow gum and wallpaper paste
and put them to my head.
He could only reach the back so
that is where he displayed his artistry –
snip, snip, snip – bald.
He rolled my deep, black, crunchy curls
around in his hand,
as if playing with a kitten.
Tired with the "pet",
he took the glue
and stuck them back.

KISS CHASE

Closed my eyes, stuck out my lips
like Sophia Loren in the films
that Mum watched on the telly –
me, behind the sofa, sneak-a-peak.

My pout ached as I waited, patient,
sucked them back in again, then ran off,
pretending that I was trying
to catch a butterfly or 'fairy'.

Girls ran around the playground, screaming,
trying to be caught. Debbie slowed down
as Jonathan caught her, hugged her –
and tried to kiss her on the lips.

She screamed, then giggled, pushed him aside.
Laughing, he went running after Jane
and caught her too. She wriggled away.
Wish he would run after me!

Once, I let Pudding Davey catch me.
But everyone ran faster than him.

RING-A-ROSES

Palm down right, palm up left,
fingers pressed firmly into Mary's hand.

She turns her head and smiles, right,
she turns and pokes her tongue out, left.

"Blackie," she mouths at me,
then smiles at the teacher.

She lets go, wipes her palm on her skirt,
looks at it, grabs mine again – tightly,

then digs her nails into the back
of my hand. I screw-up my eyes 'cos,

I don't want the teacher (or Mary),
to see me cry. She puts her head down,

quick as a rat, and sinks her teeth
into my arm. I bite back.

We all fall down.

WHITE PEOPLE CAN'T COOK RICE

Mum tried many times to show Real Mum
how to knit, how to crochet,
but she was always fingers and thumbs.
She shook her head, did Mum, at this fat-fingered African girl.

Real Mum tried many times to show Mum
how to cook rice, jollof style,
but it was always crispy, undercooked or burnt.
She sighed, did Real Mum, white people can't steam rice.

MEAL TIMES

Breakfast:
cornflakeswithmilk
bacon
sausagesbakedbeans
mushrooms
eggontoastormargandjam

or

kanya
binchakara
fufuwitplassas
jollofwit
beefchickensavourypepeyabbasentomatisstew

Dinner:
fishandchips
vinegar
applecrumble
custard
roastbeefroastpotatoesYorkshirepuddingprocessedpeasandgravy

or

kanya
binchakara
fufuwitplassas
jollofwit
beefchickensavourypepeyabbasentomatisstew

LIVING IN A LEGOLAND

Hands covered in dried pastry bits,
abruptly halted in her flow of making
rhubarb crumble for tea,

washed them, quickly, shook them,
wiped them dry on her floral pinny before
shuffling up the stairs in floppy slippers.

Hauled herself up using the banister
to move quicker than usual – then down,
careful to place both feet on each step.

Arms and chest weighed down with clothes,
I noticed my yellow "hair" cardi –
a sleeve flopped over her elbow;

dumped all on the settee. Back she went –
no stopping Mum when she was determined.
(I must get that from her).

Ken and Barbie came down next,
fighting for position with "Commando".
Lego and Lesney fell through fingers.

Crying wasn't going to help this time.
Best wait till Dad gets home
Then everything would be alright.

THE CRASHING OF LEGOLAND

Sitting on the settee, clothes heaped next to me,
I listen for the triple click of the swollen back door.

I outrun my brother into the kitchen,
tripping over the curled corner of lino on the way.

I landed face first on Dad's boot.
I sat on his foot, arms clasped below his knee,

not for my ride around the house this time,
but to stop him from moving.

My brother, too big for his other leg,
climbed onto the wobbly table to jump on Dad's back.

In our heads, unspoken but knowing each other:
"If he stays in the kitchen, then so can we."

Dad put his hands underneath my armpits, lifted me off,
not to swing high, but just about nose level.

Unspoken, but knowing each other, the words:
"If they say they want you back, you have to go."

I stopped the tears. You know how the saying goes:
"Love and hate are two sides of the same coin?"

BANISTER

Over the fence
into our house,
seeing our banister,
still brown,
still scratched,
still sturdy,

carrying the memories
of battles won –
using balustrades
to hoist up to the landing
for the bathroom race;
of battles lost –
when my Angela
was tossed over
to the squall of,
"That's the last!
No more cheek!
Get outta my 'ouse!"
from an angry
working-class mum
who fast clicked
knitpurl, knitpurl, knitpurl
into rainbow jumpers,
who didn't know,
didn't care where
Africa was…
who just wanted
to love us kids.

No point in tears
because no matter
how fast they flow,
pain is like air,

invisible yet loaded
with particles
you will never see.

WHAT'S BLOOD GOT TO DO WITH IT?

I respect my mother
but do I love her?
It's a tough one.
Which one?

I respect my mother.
She tries not to interfere.
She tries to be supportive.
She tries to be my best friend.

But do I love her?
As children
we had two,
one black, one white.

It's a tough one.
Is a mother
the one who gives birth to you
or the one who looks after you?

I respect my mother
but do I love her?
It's a tough one.
Which one?

What's blood got to do with it?

BLACK MOTHER/WHITE MOTHER

"Your mother's here,
Zainab dear,
come and show her your painting.
Don't look confused,"
teacher said, bemused.
"Why are you hesitating?"

Zainab stepped forward,
a little awkward,
and looked up at her mother.
She took her hand
walked to the easel stand
then dived away for cover.

A nervous laugh,
an embarrassed cough,
Mum dragged her from under the table.
"Here, give me a kiss,
you've really been missed."
But Zainab was not able.

A woman rushed in
amid this din,
Zainab ran to her, pleading.
"What's the problem, love,
my little dove?"
Her mother, hurt, started leaving.

Teacher's mouth dropped,
her mother stopped,
a guilt-voiced Mrs Ranger:
"I'm terribly sorry,
everybody,
Zizi's just not used to strangers."

Her mother smarted,
grabbed her arm and started
to drag Mrs R. from the classroom.
"You'll pay for this!"
Zainab's mother hissed
"This child came from my womb!"

"You've stolen her from me!"
She spat out bitterly,
"Well, she hasn't seen you for ages!"
The onslaught of words
was loudly heard
like tigers snapping across cages.

Three weeks on
to another home,
and Zainab talked to no-one.
She refused food, too,
unless cooked by one she knew,
Zainab's world was undone.

That painting was left,
like her mother, bereft
of any maternal feeling.
"MY FAMILY"
Mum, Mummy; Dad, Daddy –
black features; white faces peeling.

WEDDING PHOTOGRAPH

I
Bride in white dress against pale white skin, natural blonde hair piled
into a beehive. Groom in dark suit, black hair, almost as black as my
skin. The dark spot next to Ann – by the bride's knee – that's me.

The cameraman wasn't used to just how black black could be. My teeth
and whites of my eyes shone out! My little sis ran in front of the bride to
stand next to Mum – caught in a whisk of a moment.

My brother's face a shadow of black in his blue suit. That was almost the
end, though we didn't know it then. Maybe it was that wedding that
heralded more than a family celebration.

II
Bridesmaids dressed in sweetshop, melt-in-the-mouth colours –
sherbert in flying saucers. Pink satin with bows on our chests – the
others – one in green, one yellow – next door neighbour and best friend.

Hamandtomatacheesenpicklespambeefandchickensandwiches
crispsnpeanutsantwigletsandfairycakes
– for the party after –

non stop cola with wedding cake – bottle of bubbly for bride and groom
– elders preferred tea. Mum had her Snowball –
custard drink with lemonade.

III
Ann and I laughed over these photos – all that colour in black and white
– but went quiet as our eyes and fingers rested on the father of the
bride. He passed away a few years back.

"Dad walked the streets of London looking for you's lot. Everytime you's were deep in his head, he'd take the bus up to 'The Smoke' and just walked — came back more lopsided than ever!"

"Why did you never call us?" I couldn't answer that, so didn't even try. I offered Ann a Cadbury's Chocolate Button instead. Munched them all without speaking. His favourites.

PART III

AN AFRICAN HOUSE

THIS HOUSE IS AN AFRICAN HOUSE

This house is an African house.
This your body is an African woman's body.
This your vagina is an African woman's vagina.
All three, you keep clean, you hear?

Otherwise I will wash you out
with bleach, scrub between your legs
with a scouring pad, then I will take your body
and clean the house with it.

At eleven years old I didn't want a woman's body.
I was sure my friends didn't have vaginas
and I wanted to be just like them.
They weren't from Africa either.

CUTTING

Your grandmother was cut;
your mother was cut;
your older sister was cut.

Born in UK,
raised in UK,
schooled in UK.

No passing through puberty,
no transition;
no *bundu* to take charge of you.

If you want the respect;
if you want the wealth;
if you want to save

the honour of your mother –
we must take these blades and cut,
yes… First we throw you open

to expose your soft insides;
tender now;
slit to make you

more tender later;
knot you up like tie-dye;
unravel you slowly once the colour has set.

Because, until you bleed, you are not a woman.

TOWEL TRESSES

My dream was
to wrap my hair in a towel,
twist it turban-like and after washing fling it so that
my long tresses wouldn't drip down my back.

I put my hands in my hair,
tugged it to stretch it out,
still couldn't see it out of the corner of my eye.
What kind of girl was I?

ADORING MICHAEL

If Michael ever gets to meet me,
he'll fall madly in love with me,
I *know* dat.
Born the same year,
same height, same colour –
see me, with my Afro too,
so we're match perfect.
In time, we'll get married,
have four children; two boys; two girls.
I love Michael and I know,
if he could just be allowed to meet me,
he'll fall in love with me!

It's tough loving a star;
they have so many girls after them
(and some days I think it might just be better
to love Marlon instead),
but when Michael sings,
"Ain't No Sunshine",
I know he's singing just for me.

I know everything about him:
His zodiac sign: Virgo.
(We're compatible.)
His favourite colours:
red, black, silver, and gold.
(Mine too.)

His favourite food:
Mexicanspicyandvegetarian
sushipizzachickenfishfreshfruits
popcornvanillaicecreamwithcookiepieces
sunflowerseedsglazeddoughnuts
frostedflakeswithmilkM&Ms.
(Mine too.)

Michael and his brothers got
their own cartoon show
before the Osmonds!
I get up early Sat'day mornings
to do my house chores
so that my mum will let me watch it.
She just don't understand that
when he sings, "Got To Be There"
it don't mean Tesco's
and washing windows – don't mean jack!

Michael can dance too, guy!
We feel sorry for the white girls dem at school
'cos there's *no way* Donny and his brothers
could be as cool as the Jackson Five!

His eyes hook into mine
from the poster on my bedroom wall
where I can dream about him
at home, and at school where
his cut-out pictures from
Jackie magazine are stuck
on my Maths and English books,
from where he shines like the star
that he always will be.

IN STITCHES

She was like purl,
smooth and sophisticated; never disrupted the pattern or flow;
neat and pleasant to look at.

My self a knit,
rough where it was not welcome; mistakes always visible,
jutted out and always turned over.

Always trying to be more like purl,
ending up crossing, more like cable –
chunky, spiralling too fast.

Despair and frustration,
not knowing how to control 90 to 270 –
the wayward stitches grew on their own!

An ungainly body of work.
Maybe as I grow older, my knit might look as pretty as purl
and I could own it, with confidence.

FROM PRINT TO SCRIPT

I was comfortable in my round printedness;
safe and secure, my prowess was clear.
But when my father saw my lines
he said nothing for a while,
disappointment, obvious on his face.
He was committed to changing me overnight.

From "print" to "script"
until my disjointedness curved
and the fast track of growing up
left a girl behind who didn't know
whether she was best in print,
or taking her time to learn script –
although really, she had no choice.

NAMED FOR HER

Sheer.
Black.
Laddered.
Woven tight.
Into cornrows.
Ear to ear.
Forehead to nape.
Sectioned like a hot-cross bun.
Parted to show a caramelled brown surface
where the sun works with hair grease to
moisten the curly edges that shape her forehead,
brightening her face from matt to slightly shiny.

"That's my mum's face you have there."
I grinned and silently thanked Granny for being beautiful.

RICE

The first time I went "back home", I returned with country rice,
small grains that sifted like tiny diamonds,
coarse and flecked with variant browns like gravel,
not like the "own brand" that sheds milky-white starch into water,
long grained, fluffy and soft, that we eat on Sunday afternoons.

But Mum said, "I don't cook that unpolished rice anymore,"
and threw it away. A bit like our language.

PINK SHOES

Pink shoes. First ones.
Wedge heel. Silver buttons.
At forty, not four years old.

My foot steps in easy
like Cinderella's,
'cept there were no
fairy-tale princesses
black like me in my storybooks,
like there were
no pink shoes, when I was four.

Red dress. First one.
Polka dots. Sleeveless.
At four months, not four years old.

My father walked fourteen miles
to work, for four weeks,
in 1962. His first snow,
because he spent his
tuppence bus money
on a red dress
for his "*Pretty* (Devil) Woman".

Now I'm 40
and I will wear
pink shoes. Pink lipstick.
Pink nails. With stars.

And a red dress too.

SKIPPING

Two girls holding
one each end of the rope
always tripped me up on "plate".

Customs Officer holding
my British passport
always tripped me up at the gate.

I tried to dip out faster,
but they would twist the rope
faster still – so I never won.

I tried an extra-wide smile,
at the British citizens' queue
watched my passport swiped by infra red.

I stood aside and watched –
they never did it to anyone else.

I stood aside and watched –
they never did it to anyone else.

PART 4

HOMELAND

KISSY STREET

Her voice cracks through the hymns in Methodist,
in her one, narrow-brimmed, Sunday straw hat;
underneath, hair folded into curved shapes like plantain.

She wears one of her two Sunday dresses,
small floral print as "discovered" by Laura Ashley,
pleated into her narrow waist.

She won't leave her house; she won't leave her verandah;
she won't leave the contentment of the home where she knows
each place setting of tiny pebbles and stones in the eight steps of cement;

eight steps that lead to her home of eighty-five years;
three hus-bands, five child-ren and one sis-tah of eighty-three years
separated only by a wall of chipboard painted cream turned yellow…

And alternating breaths – her same breath she takes
to pray, give thanks – she translates and sings
all this into her own hymn.

"Kerr me go Inglan? Mmm-mmm – tenki ya but
ar noh go lef me ose foh no-bo-dy – no sah.
Di only tem ar go lef dis contry,
na foh meet wit God Almighty."

SHOOTS

Sapling legs bend smoothly, power foot in place,
her back, parallel to solid ground,
makes her torso a table of support.

"Es yusef na me back; I ge fo carry yu, me pikin."

I'm unconvinced – my thick calves dangle;
heavy breasts squashed-up against the shoulders
of her five-foot one-and-a half inch frame.

Her thinned breasts, ridged, matured,
hang like sappos from a tree
as they droop, dried.

Forward leaning, her torso supports
my legs for one – less than one – minute,
me, afraid our bonding may break her,

but her drive leg is ready to spring back, as I slide off,

now knowing it is Granny's legs each
time I'm ready to take off when I'm on my marks
to get ready, get set, and go!

WELCOME TO ENGLAND

One day, "she's coming",
the next, "she's here".

So far away for so long,
bringing her to us, across the Atlantic,

does not close the sea gap
of no cakes, no hugs.

I went to visit her at my parents' house
to kiss her hands, welcome her to England.

She smiled; a vague recognition
with her tiny, brown-toothed smile.

I carried her, on my back,
to sitting room warmth.

The situation now in reverse.

GRANDMOTHERS II

I

Small as my hand, her face
holds grey-brown pebble eyes;
lips small, round and brown like a lychee seed.

Wrapped in blanketsearmuffslegwarmersknittedhat –
crimplene trousers with sewn-in pleats,
browny-beige from M&S like her daughter wore.

She talked… much,
but we did not understand Mende.
Her chatter was a cry to go home.

II

She spoke… little,
wanting only to chew her *pe-pe*.
and her stick to keep her teeth strong.

Wrapped in overripemangoesrottenplantainburnt*crao* –
rich red-brown palm oil – that colours the meeting of teeth.
The scent of a well-worn, difficult life.

Narrow as my hand, her face
holds eyes that dart, switch side to side,
day and night, like the geckos that scratch her roof.

QUEEN OF OL' WHARF

(for Grandma Adama)

I

From her chair that rocks
on the verandah, she surveys her empire.

In her chair she rocks,
squelches tidbits of rice and fish

into a ball in her right palm
rolls it to the tip of

two fingers and broad thumb
flattened by years of threading hair,

pushes them one by one onto the waiting
tongues of her army of toddlers.

Once she is sure that are all fed
and they run off to play in dirt and sun,

she rinses her hands, prays, naps,
wakes to the gentle laps of life,

waits for the envelope her son must bring
each month from her daughter in England

to keep her in the last days of her reign,
to keep her in rice and *pe-pe* fish balls.

II

Yet this son of her land arrives with no
blue-inked white-envelope

but with black gun, peppering bullets
into the four-year-old with hand in hers –

puppy fat falls away
from
        soft
                wrinkled
                        wisdom.

Grandma can't hold off boys
who come with stones and bullets

instead of homemade nets, fish hooks
curved from spokes of abandoned bikes;

boys who run fast-fast to keep Grandma Wharf
safe, who run from where they swim

shot
    in
        their
                footsteps.

III

Green-skinned orange trees, pale pink bell-apples
sugar-laden grapefruit sheltered Grandma's

two-bed corrugated steel-roofed house
with personal borehole and latrine,

secluded in the valleyed curve
away from the daily life of

oil-fuming cars, hailing conductors that
barrages her nostrils and ears.

Why do men at war fear the poor,
convinced that enemies hide in their homes;

forcing women to torch their men,
ordering boys to kill their grandmas,

laughing, as they hide, scared,
until they can flee into refugee zones?

FOUND…

...on a bed of domestic garbage –
cans, bottles, rags, ring-pulls, bottle tops,

rotten fishheads, serrated lids, jagged meal tops,
flips without their flops – mulched thick into a mattress.

Through months of rain and months of sun
that soaked, then baked her clothes to her body;

denying her the ritual of burial within 24 hours:
this was how my grandmother was found.

THE STORY OF THE GLOBE

Outside.
Olde-worlde brown skin,
embossed with Latin and Olde-English gnarled and twisted font.
Our fingers flattened and applied pressure,
pushing it to spin heavily on a crooked axis.

Inside.
Chivers Scotch whisky, sweet Sherry
and cans of Carlsberg lager.
Cut-glass decanters wearing their own necklace labels.
Underneath, a tray held tins of salted, roasted peanuts and twiglets.

Ornamental.
Our globe drinks cabinet was
pride of the sitting room, so we spun it in secret,
but never found Sierra Leone.
And now that we have, its romance remains on the skin of the globe.

THE REALITY OF THE ATLAS

"A people without the knowledge of their past History, origin and culture is like a tree without roots."

— Marcus Garvey Jr.

"If you don't know where you are going, you might wind up someplace else."
— Yogi Berra

"Here is Africa; here is the West Indies and all this here is England."

I come from somewhere in between.
This picture of the world is so huge
that I'm not exactly sure where my place is
on the map, in the world, even in my classroom.

Real Mum and Dad say we are from
someplace called Sierra Leone which means mountain lion in Italian,
named by a Portuguese explorer. As a ship sails in to port,
the mountain looks as though two lions are facing you.

"You look like a Ja - mai - can?"
But don't we all look the same —
dark skin/thick hair/full lips/curved bums.
I trace my family tree and it lands in — Barbados!

And what of England? Where I was born, raised and schooled?
Which has taught me nothing of Africa, of the West Indies.
That showed me a map of the world without me,
or my real mum and dad.

"Where do I come from? Africa, Barbados, England — all three?"

NO PLANS TO RETURN

I

"They came with photos," he said,
"of an England we had never seen —
sun, in Hyde Park.

They told us they would help
with a place to live,
a job! If I went, I could

look after my mum,
my sister with crook leg
who never married.

Now, our children here
are trapped. No jobs;
no homes; no way out.

We are old now, going soon.
We thought we had built
a foundation for them

during Thatcher's rule
but they're not benefiting.
Told to go back home,

just as we were —
over fifty years ago —
just as we were…"

II

"You lied to my papa!" she said.
"You told him,
'Everything will be fine.'

We would have a dry place to live,
a kitchen for me to cook,
a bed to sleep in.

And true enough
you provided all of those.
But you did not supply love.

This country is lonely
when you no get
famble na ya!

Me, I'm ready
to return home
where things are not perfect

but where it is warm,
people are friendly,
and my skin is not a sin."

III

"We don't talk about these times," he said,
"they've passed. We came to
better our lives; better our selves,

take care of family back home —
the never ending family that
swells with each monthly cheque!

This has become a tiresome life.
Nothing is moving,
no-one is progressing.

So I've decided,
that when I'm ready,
what I'm going to do

is to say to my wife,
'I don't want to live anymore.'
We will lie on our bed,

hold hands and drift away.
My one wish is
that we go together.

I brought her here,
she should leave with me.
Maybe it's time to let go...

...We have no plans to return."

IV

No plans to return home.
We are old now, used
to this way of life.

My eyes are failing me.
I can still see fine
but if it gets worse…

I don't trust their WHO medicine.
If my wife gets sick,
where do I get help

to take her to hospital?
If her other hip goes,
I can't lift her alone.

Maybe, when they get electric,
we'll reconsider. When I left,
everything ran – perfectly.

Now, neither gas nor petrol,
no clean water, no rice!
I hear: "*Gi we light!*"

It is as if colonialism
was our saviour, political independence
our assassin, economic independence –

Satan. Were Africans not the
first people on this earth?
Yet look at us now?

We live as though we'll
be the first to go!
Have we no pride left?

We gave the British PM
our highest honour – Paramount Chief,
but – his embarrassment, our shame –

he refused our bogolan robes.
The world saw it all.
We have not moved on.

We've thrown ourselves back into
captivity; never left mental slavery.
We've no plans to return.

TEMPORARY HOMES

In England, you could always tell where black folks lived.
Houses painted baby-pink, sky-blue, marigold-yellow,
colourful, welcoming, smiling – brightening their spirits,
warming their chilled bones (the only way to get through the winter of '62).
These are their homes, until they can return to their homeland.

In Egypt, we approached Elephantine Island by boat.
Houses of mint-green, strawberry-ice cream, daffodil-yellow,
embossed with alligators and the yellow flowers of friendship.
They sit unsettled in hills and along the shore cut off before the Dam.
These are their homes, until they can return to their homeland.

And these are my people; from the same continent; from the same breath.

GLOSSARY AND NOTES

p. 11   **Wit Krio titi ar no say –** If she was a Krio girl, I would know that

oos – which

p. 42   **pe-pe** – pepper

yabbas – onion

binch – beans – **binch akara** – like a small fried bean dumpling (usually made with black eyed beans)

fufu – made from starchy root vegetables into a thick 'paste'. Eaten like pounded yam or sadza with 'plassas'

plassas – greens – A stew (fish/meat) made with palm oil and greens such as cassava leaves, potato leaves, crain-crain. In the UK this can also be substituted with spinach

kanya – a snack made with groundnuts, flour and sugar. Looks like crumble

p. 56   **bundu** – (also known as sande), a women's 'secret society' to initiate girls into womanhood

p. 64   "Pretty (Devil) Woman" – refers to the song by Roy Orbison

p. 69   **kerr me go –** carry me (take me to)

tenki ya – thank you

os – house

p. 70   **es yusef –** hoist yourself (climb)

sappo – commonly called a loofah

p. 72   **crao** – rice at the bottom of the pot which often goes crispy/hard

p. 80.   **famble** – family

ABOUT THE AUTHOR

Kadija Sesay is a graduate of Birmingham University (with a major in West African Studies). She is the founder/publisher of SABLE LitMag, and SABLE LitFest. She is co-director of the Inscribe programme for Professional Development for Peepal Tree Press and the series editor for their Inscribe imprint. Their first anthology is *Red: Contemporary Black British Poetry* (2010). Their second forthcoming anthology of fiction will be *Closure*. She has edited several groundbreaking anthologies of work by writers of African and Asian descent, the latest being, *Dreams Miracles and Jazz: New Adventures in African Fiction* (Picador Africa, 2008) edited with Helon Habila. Other anthologies include, *Dance the Guns to Silence: 100 Poems for Ken Saro-Wiwa* (with Nii Ayikwei Parkes) *and IC3: The Penguin Book of New Black Writing in Britain* (with Courttia Newland) and *Write Black, and Write British: From Post Colonial to Black British Literature.* She is also an Associate Editor for *Callaloo*, the premier journal of arts, letters, and cultures of the African Diaspora.

Kadija has co-ordinated various literary events, such as "Word from Africa" at the British Museum (2008) and organises international writer's residencies – the SABLE Writer's HotSpot to The Gambia, Cuba and New York. She is also an accredited life coach and an Associate with Vision Quest International.

Kadija is an award recipient for her work in the creative arts, namely: Cosmopolitan Woman of Achievement (1994), Candice magazine Woman of Achievement (1996), Voice Newspaper Award for work in the Creative Arts (1998) and a Woman of the Millennium (2000). In 2001-2002, she completed the inaugural year of the Vilar Fellowship in Performing Arts Management at the J.F. Kennedy Center for Performing Arts in Washington, DC. She is a George Bell Fellow and General Secretary for the PEN African Writer's Abroad Centre and a founding member of PAN (PEN African Writers Network). She received a STAR Award (2006), a reward for Sierra Leoneans for their service in the community.

www.kadijasesay.com; www.sableltimag.org

www.discoveryourfuture.wordpress.com

PRAISE FOR *IRKI*

Irki examines the cultural interior of a woman coming of age. Kadija Sesay pulls us into Europe without forgetting Africa. There are many sides to blackness and one size doesn't fit all. Sesay's words are capable of creating a home. Place this book next to what you are eating. There is no longer a reason to be hungry. Because of Kadija we can finally say grace.

E. Ethelbert Miller
Director, African American Resource Center
Howard University, Washington, D.C

This is marvellous verse. Why did she spend so much time doing other irrelevant things instead of writing poetry? I must get back to these poems – they are so meaningful! Go on, give us another volume!

Jack Mapanje, *The Beasts of Nalunga*

Witty and energetic, Kadija Sesay's poems come alive with the pulsating rhythms and smells of childhood and the clear, scalpel-like reflections of the adult complexities faced by a sensitive and keen-eyed woman in multicultural Britain.

Syl Cheney-Coker, Award winning author of *The Last Harmattan of Alusine Dunbar.*

I know Kadija as a brilliant & helpful editor, making a great contribution to our modern literature & culture, but i've nvr seen her poetry until now – tho i've often asked her about it and don't even know if this is her first book of verse! – it "feels" like an "early" work – ?surprisingly "direct", dealing w/ 'Black British Woman issues, especially in this case GROWING UP inc "Two Mothers" ("What's Blood got to do with it") and of course "'Air" and things like Food and Dad and Family and finally a visit Home to Sierra Leone (see "This House is an African House"). But mainly this is very "early" Kadija – good to begin at the Beginning! – but we also dying to hear of the Kadija we now know & love – the Kadija of the poem w/its kaiso title, "Skipping"

Kamau Brathwaite 14 July 2012